Ephphatha! Open Up!

A Children's Curriculum For Understanding Disabilities

**Disabilities In Ministry Committee
Of The North Indiana Conference
Of The United Methodist Church**

CSS Publishing Company, Inc., Lima, Ohio

Dedicated to Betty Stewart, whose vital spirit and visionary leadership has given hope to many and birth to the Disabilities in Ministry Committee of the North Indiana Conference.

ISBN 0-7880-1350-5   PRINTED IN U.S.A.

Ephphatha

(Ef-fa'-tha)
Mark 7:34
"Open Up"

A curriculum written for students in grades 3 through 6.

In the book of Mark (7:34) Jesus says, "*Ephphatha* — Open Up" — and things happened.

In these lessons, children will begin to OPEN UP to persons with disabilities and will recognize their positive abilities. In return, persons with disabilities will OPEN UP and see ways they can use their potentials. Opening up awareness to the gifts within each of us will expand the use of our God-given talents.

Northern Indiana Conference
Committee on Disabilities in Ministries

July 1996

EPHPHATHA lessions prepared by:

The Disabilities in Ministries Committee
North Indiana Conference
United Methodist Church

1996

Carol and David Black
Galveston, Indiana

Dr. Ralph Karstedt
Bremen, Indiana

Nancy and Harold Bradley
Hammond, Indiana

Verna Neidigh
Bremen, Indiana

Rev. Sherrie Drake
Muncie, Indiana

Rev. Tim Powers
Morocco, Indiana

Rev. Robert Jarboe
Huntington, Indiana

Dr. Joe Smith
Kentland, Indiana

Betty Stewart, Chairman
Plymouth, Indiana

Acknowledgments

Sherrie Drake
General Editor

William Stofer
Final Editor

Bill Drake
Computer Layout

Suzanne Mades
Special Article

"EPHPHATHA" (Ef-fa'-tha) is the healing word spoken by Jesus in Mark 7:34. It is a strong command which is translated "OPEN UP!"

In Mark's story, a man is given new possibilities for life as his ears are opened and the blessings of hearing and speech are restored to him. The end result of the miracle is that the gathered crowd sees and understands the remarkable power of Jesus and the foundation for belief is laid.

EPHPHATHA acts in many ways. It invites us to open up ourselves to the warm humanity within physically limited people. It also challenges the disabled to OPEN UP themselves and take advantage of their God-given strengths and abilities.

The life of Jesus was a constant challenge to all who met him to "open up" their thinking, "open up" their feelings, and to "open up" their being to new ways of life through his power.

Our goal with this curriculum is that you will be able to challenge your class to "open up" to the possibilities of understanding, accepting, and valuing the special gifts given to us as children of God. In so doing, you will be following the path of the Teacher of all teachers, Jesus.

We wish you joy in the journey.

Members of the North Indiana Conference
United Methodist Church
Committee on Disabilities in Ministry

A Note To Teachers And Pastors

EPHPHATHA! is written as a series of thirteen Sunday School lessons, with a brief bibliography of additional resources at the end of the publication. It is our intention that teachers take great liberty in tailoring the curriculum to meet the needs of their classes.

Invert, throw out, add to, rearrange the sessions so that your students will gain the maximum learning experience. Utilize additional resources, especially "living resources" if you are fortunate enough to have them in your church. No one will be able to explain "blindness" to children better than someone who lives day in and day out with that situation! Experiment with using these materials at times other than Sunday mornings — maybe in kids' clubs or fellowship gatherings, maybe in intergenerational settings.

In addition, we strongly encourage you to look at the worship materials provided at the end of the sessions. It may be that your class can work with a worship committee to design a worship experience for the whole congregation.

We thank you in advance for your dedication to children and their possibilities. Our prayer is that through these lessons, children will begin to "Open Up!" to persons with disabilities and will recognize their positive abilities; and that persons with disabilities will "Open Up!" to an awareness of new ways in which they can use their potentials.

We commend these thoughts to you in the name of the One who looks at each of us and commands, "Ephphatha! Open up!"

Table Of Contents

Session:

1. Alike Or Different?   9

2. Looking At Blindness   15

3. Looking At Blindness II   19

4. Understanding Physical Handicaps   27

5. Understanding Physical Handicaps II   31

6. Deafness And Hearing Impairment   35

7. Communication   39

8. "Slow" And "Stupid" Are *Not* The Same   42

9. Kindness Is Always In Order   45

10. How Does It Feel? How Can We Help?   51

11. Let's Look At Us   55

12. What Does It Mean To Be Healed?   57

13. Receive This Gift ...   59

Extra Activity   61

Additional Resources   63

Resources For Worship   65

Session 1
Alike Or Different?
by Verna S. Neidigh

PURPOSE:

1. To help children become aware that God loves each person individually, no matter how different one person may be from another.

2. To help children accept and treat persons with disabilities in a compassionate manner.

MATERIALS:

    Chalk and chalkboard
    Newsprint chart
    Markers
    Bibles
    Copies of the skit, *A Giant Step In Understanding* (at least six)
    Six signs for skit: ELEVATOR, EXIT, HALL, CLASSROOM, STAIRWAY, LIBRARY

PROCEDURE:

Begin with prayer for opening hearts and minds to treating persons with disabilities as Jesus would — lovingly.

Ask class members to help you list ways in which they are 1) alike, and 2) different. Display list on chalkboard or newsprint chart.

Example

	Alike	Different
Human beings	X	
One head each	X	
Ten fingers each	X	
Need for love/security	X	
Names		X
Eye color		X
Hair color		X
Height		X
Weight		X
Food likes		X
Gender		X
Race		X
Nationality		X
Hobbies/Interests		X

DISCUSSION:

1. We are alike in some ways, different in others.

2. Do you think our differences keep God from loving any of us? (*John 3:16*)

3. Do you think our differences should keep us from loving God? (*Matthew 22:37, 38*)

4. Do you think our differences should keep us from loving each other, as well as others, even our enemies? (*Matthew 22:39; Luke 6:27; Galatians 6:10*)

SKIT:
A Giant Step In Understanding

Choose volunteers to portray the characters Sam, Curly, Sally, Bud, Brett, and Tess. Other children can work on setting the classroom with impromptu "sets" and "props" while the readers are looking through the script together.

Allow time for guided discussion following the skit, encouraging children in their reactions to the characters and the change that occurred in Tess once she allowed herself to get to know Sally. (Some additional material to guide your discussion is included in the separate Discussion Guideline.)

CLOSING:
End with prayer of thanksgiving that God loves all of us, no matter how different we may be one from another.

Skit For Session 1

A Giant Step In Understanding
Adapted by
Verna S. Neidigh

A two-act play adapted from a true story as told by Virginia J. Risica in her article, "A Giant Step in Understanding," *Guideposts Magazine*, copyright 1994 by Guideposts Associates, Inc., Carmel, New York 10512.

Characters:

 Six children, school peers (in order of appearance in ACT 1)

Sam and **Curly**, students who haven't learned to be courteous to persons with disabilities

Sally, the *shortest* character and a new student, suffers from juvenile rheumatoid arthritis. Her bones and joints ache; her muscles are stiff. Also, her hands and feet are deformed. Because Sally can't climb the school's stairs as fast as the other students, she uses the elevator

Bud and **Brett**, buddies who taunt Sally

Tess, the *tallest* character, looks and acts tough at first

Act 1

(Scene: The setting is in a school HALL. The STAIRWAY is at one end. The CLASSROOM is at the opposite end. Midway between, on one side, is the ELEVATOR, across from which is an EXIT. Each place is marked by an identifying sign.)

Sam and **Curly** (*carrying books in backpacks*) *are in the HALL jesting with each other...that is, until they notice the new and very different student,* **Sally**. *Laughing, they point and make faces at her as she enters the HALL from the ELEVATOR.*

Sally (*awkwardly carrying two books*) *tries to ignore* **Sam** *and* **Curly's** *rude behavior. Taking small, painful steps, she walks as normally as possible toward the CLASSROOM.*

Bud and **Brett** (*each nonchalanty carrying three or four school books tucked under an arm*) *step from the STAIRWAY to the HALL. Challenged by the strange sight of Sally, they head toward her from behind...to taunt her.*

Bud: (*sarcastically*) "Hey, who shrunk you?"

Brett: (*insultingly*) "Need a shove, kid?"

Sally, *hurting as much from the taunting as from her physical pain, doesn't respond to any of her tormentors. Instead, she continues toward the CLASSROOM while silently praying for her tormentors. To indicate the silent praying, Sally could briefly close her eyes, lightly touch both hands together, and/or slightly bow her head.*

Sam, **Curly**, **Bud**, and **Brett**, *without further incident, quietly leave the HALL at the EXIT, as...*

Tess *(easily carrying three or four school books) exits the STAIRWAY to enter the HALL. Startled by the sight of **Sally** farther down the hall, **Tess** hesitates before striding up beside Sally.*

Tess: *(staring down at Sally)* "What are you doing here? How old *are* you?"

Sally: *(drawing herself up as if "standing up inside" answers firmly)* "You don't frighten me! I'm ten, same as you, but I wasn't born as lucky."

Tess *(visibly softened) swoops up Sally's books to carry with her own.*

Tess *and* **Sally** *walk together to CLASSROOM...at **Sally's** slower pace.*

Act 2

(Scene: Several months later. The setting is an ELEVATOR opening onto the school LIBRARY, which contains a table and two chairs. Each place is marked by an identifying sign.)

Tess *and* **Sally** *are riding in the elevator. The two friends are on their way to study together in the LIBRARY. Tess carries four books, both her own and **Sally's**.*

Sally: *(gratefully)* "Tess, you've helped me so much this year!"

Tess: *(surprised, but pleased)* "Well, what have I done?"

Sally: *(thoughtfully)* "Oh, for one thing, every day you've carried my books! Also, you've been so good about getting things for me when I couldn't reach them. What would I have done without you?"

Tess: *(delightedly)* "Oh, you're welcome! I've loved helping you! Besides, we've become friends. How about all the help you've given me with my homework? What would I have done without you?"

Sally: "Well, we *have* helped each other, haven't we? I'm so thankful you're my friend. Now, let's get busy! We have tests tomorrow."

Tess moves an arm to indicate that the ELEVATOR door is opening.

Tess and **Sally** (*both smiling*) *enter the LIBRARY.* **Tess** *places all their books on the table.* **Tess** *and* **Sally** *settle down on chairs next to each other at the table. Each spreads open a book and begins to study.*

The End

Discussion Guideline

for

Session 1 Skit

A Giant Step In Understanding

Coping With Disability

Sally was not only new in school, she was also "different" from her peers in appearance, height, and physical abilities. For instance, Sally could neither walk at a normal pace nor use the stairway. Nevertheless, she coped, or managed well.

What were some of Sally's coping methods?

Ask the class to help you list a few on chalkboard or newsprint.

You may consider the following examples:

    1. Sally couldn't use the stairway. How did she reach her classroom and the library? *[By an alternative method, the elevator.]*

    2. Sally felt hurt by being taunted by Sam, Curly, Bud, and Brett. How did she handle her hurt? *[By silently praying for taunters.]*

    3. Sally couldn't reach far or high enough. How did she get things she couldn't reach? *[By accepting Tess's help.]*

    4. Sally appreciated Tess's help. How did she let Tess know? *[By thanking her.]*

    5. Sally didn't concentrate on what she couldn't do. She did what she *could* do. How did she demonstrate that? *[By helping Tess with her homework; by being willing to persevere.]*

Sally isn't the only character in the play who coped with her disabilities. Point out to the class that Tess also changed as a result of getting to know Sally; she also coped with Sally's disabilities. Discuss and list Tess's behavior, such as the following:

    1. When Tess first saw Sally, did Tess cope, or did she react rudely? *[The latter.]*

    2. What did Tess do when Sally responded assertively? *[She changed her own attitude.]*

    3. How did Tess's attitude show? *[By her thoughtful actions and examples.]*

    4. What if you were Tess?

        a. What would you do when you saw Bud and Brett teasing Sally?

        b. Do things like this happen in you church or school?

        c. Could they happen? If so, how would you handle them?

Session 2
Looking At Blindness
by Harold and Nancy Bradley

This session and the one which follows are designed to explore the issue of blindness and some of the adaptive technology that has been developed which allows blind people to function more easily. This session deals with some of the specific technology. The following session focuses more on our own attitudes toward those who are blind.

It is highly recommended that you invite a blind guest to speak and explain directly the adaptive devices that he or she has chosen to use in his or her own life. Session 3 focuses more on our own attitudes toward those who are blind. You may wish to invert the order of the lessons according to the scheduling availability of your guest.

If you do not have access to a blind speaker, the following information has been prepared so that you can speak to your class about some of the technology which is currently available. In addition, you may wish to check with local hospitals or schools for the blind for resources. The North Indiana Conference Media Resource Center has film and video suggestions. Information on Leader Dogs for the Blind can be obtained from your local Lions Club or by writing directly to Leader Dogs for the Blind, 1039 South Rochester Road, P.O. Box 5000, Rochester, MI 48307, (313) 651-9011.

PURPOSE:
To introduce students to some of the many ways blind people adapt to a primarily sighted world. To raise consciousness about the nature of blindness.

MATERIALS:
>Braille alphabet cards which may be purchased from American Printing House for the Blind, Library of Congress, or the American Foundation for the Blind.
>White cane
>Talking book machines and tape player may be borrowed from a machine lending agency.
>Braille writing equipment: slate and stylus, a Perkins Brailer, if possible.
>A Braille book, and a volume of the Braille Bible.

PROCEDURE:
Begin by having a class member who is comfortable with reading aloud read Matthew 9:27-31. Explain that in Jesus' time blind people had to beg and were rejected by the people around them. People were almost frightened to be around them because they were thought to have received their blindness as a punishment for their sin. Ask your students how they think it would feel to be blind if the people around them had this attitude.

Jesus taught that this was not true, and he reached out to heal these people in a way that would allow them to live well in their world. When he did this it helped everyone understand how special and powerful he was so that they could believe more deeply in him.

Although we now know that blindness has many different causes and is not something that a person needs to be ashamed of, the old negative attitude towards blind people is present today in the church and the world.

One thing that is important for children to remember is that blindness is not shameful. It is a characteristic, just like having brown hair or blue eyes. The only difference about blindness is that the blind cannot see. It is O.K. to use the word "blind," for that is what they are.

Blind people lead everyday lives. They have friends, go to school, work, ride bikes, watch television, go to the movies, cook, clean. Anything sighted people do, blind people do.

The problem for the blind is the negative attitudes that many people have toward them. Ask your students how they feel when they see a blind person. Explain that today's lesson will help them understand some of the equipment that has been developed by and for blind people so that they can function more independently.

How can a blind person...

The teacher will ask, *How do you think blind people read and write?*

Answer: They use Braille.

Braille was invented in the eighteenth century by a blind man named Louis Braille. Mr. Braille was blinded when he was a child. His father was a saddle maker, and one day Louis was playing with a sharp instrument called an awl. He accidentally struck himself in the eye, blinding that eye. The other eye became infected as a result of the wound, and Louis became totally blind. He invented the Braille system of coding books and other printed material in a form of raised dots on paper. Braille cells are now used throughout our world. They can be found in elevators, hospitals, schools, government buildings, bank teller machines, and even some McDonald's restaurants.

Blind people read and write Braille as easily as you read and write print. Each letter is formed in a shape called a "cell." A cell is rectangular and contains six dots which are numbered. Each letter of the alphabet is a different combination of dots in a cell.

Demonstration: Show class a slate and stylus.

Braille may be written with a slate and stylus. When you write with a slate and stylus, the dots are numbered going down, 1, 2, 3 on the right side of a cell, and 4, 5, 6 on the left side of the cell. Slates come in all sizes. The largest is forty cells and the smallest is a postcard slate which has nineteen cells. Most slates can fit into a pocket or purse and can be regarded as one's pen or pencil.

A Perkins Brailler is a machine with six keys and a spacebar in the middle. The dot combinations in the cell are reversed on the machine, 1, 2, 3 on the left and 4, 5, 6 on the right. Braille is written by pressing the key combinations. Braille may also be written on a computer and be printed by a Braille printer. Interested children may come and look at the equipment, perhaps use it.

Grade one Braille is all the letters in word spelled out, letter by letter. *Grade two Braille* has special code combinations for common words and word endings. *Grade three Braille* has even more individual codes to represent words and word endings.

Braille books take up a lot of space.

The teacher will ask, *How many volumes is the Braille Bible?*

Answer: Eighteen. (*Show the volume of the Braille Bible.*)

Another way blind people read is by using tape and records called flexible discs. We borrow talking book and tape players that play the tapes at a slower speed. Books are recorded at a slower speed because it uses less tape. (*Show tapes.*) Most fiction and non-fiction books are on cassette. Best sellers are on flexible disc. (*Show disc.*) Popular magazines such as *Sports Illustrated* and *U.S. News and World Report* are on disc; *Newsweek* and *Reader's Digest* are on tape. *Jack and Jill* is on disc and *My Weekly Reader* is in Braille. There is a talking book program for children's books also.

The teacher will ask, *How do blind people get around?*

Answer: There are three ways: white cane, dog guide, and sighted people. All are acceptable to blind persons.

Travel with a white cane is a skill that must be taught; the training is called *mobility instruction*. The feel and sounds of walking surfaces against the cane tip help the blind walker tell when there is a change in the sidewalk or a curb. Traffic sounds help determine when it is safe to cross the street. A blind person may choose to use a straight or folding cane.

In order to receive dog guide training, a person must be at least sixteen years of age. He or she does not have to be totally blind in order to qualify for dog guide training. There are seventeen dog guide schools in the United States and Canada. A person attends the school for thirty days. During that time, the student is matched with his or her dog and they are taught how to work as a team. The owner still needs to listen to traffic sounds in order to tell the dog where to go. It is the human, not the dog, who makes the travel commands. Sometimes the training is done from a student's home if he or she lives near the school. Some people train their own dogs. (See information about Leader Dogs for the Blind in the introductory material.)

Some blind people use a sighted guide as a form of mobility. The blind person takes the arm of a sighted person and they walk to where they are going. Sometimes the blind person also has the cane or dog, sometimes not. It is important to remember that if you are a sighted person, let the blind person take your arm. That way you are a half-step ahead. All three means of travel make the blind person independent.

The teacher will explain some other ways a blind person may adapt to his or her world:

Descriptive Video Services (DVS) is opening new horizons for the blind. DVS describes some PBS television programs and popular movies. Scenery, costumes, scene changes, and body language are all described. The verbal description does not interfere with the movie. The movies may be borrowed from libraries or purchased from Descriptive Video Services. Some described movies include *Raiders of the Lost Ark, Dumbo, Anne of Green Gables,* and *True Grit. (Show a DVS catalog.)*

Some blind people tell money apart by folding each denomination a different way.

Some blind people use watches with special faces on them that allow them to feel rather than see what time it is.

Blind people have jobs, raise families, and do household chores. Blind adults and children can be active in their churches. A blind child can acolyte and participate in a Sunday school class. The blind child can also do household chores. Being blind doesn't mean one can't do the work; it means that one may have to use different techniques to get the job done.

CLOSING:
Have the children sit or stand in a circle and invite them to tell the class one new thing they learned about ways that blind people have adapted to life in a world where most people can see. End with a prayer of thanksgiving to God for these special technologies which allow people to live their lives more independently.

Session 3
Looking At Blindness II
by Harold and Nancy Bradley

It is very important that the teacher be open to the positive attitudes about blindness in this lesson. Blind children can do all that Leslie does. The story about Leslie is intended to raise consciousness about the abilities of blind persons. You may wish to familiarize yourself with the story and tell it in your own words rather than read it. Or you may have students who are comfortable reading in front of others take turns reading the story aloud. You may also have students who would prefer to role-play the scenes.

PURPOSE:
To use a story to model some of the abilities rather than the disabilities of one blind girl as she goes about her ordinary routines with her church friends.

MATERIALS:
> A copy of the story, *Leslie Gilson* (story is too long for one session.)
> Bibles

BACKGROUND:
The following information is provided for you as a teacher to stimulate some ideas of topics which can be discussed during the reading of the story. According to the nature of your class, you may wish to read the story in sections, discussing some of these questions as you progress. These may also be used to stimulate discussion following a straight through reading. Some ideas for discussion are also included in the body of the story itself. Other ideas are puppets, drama, extra sessions.

*If you have been through **Session 2** with your class, your students will already be familiar with some of the adaptive technology mentioned in this story which allows Leslie to do things like check her watch or "read" her Bible lesson. If you are still anticipating **Session 2**, this may help lay the groundwork.*

Leslie is a blind sixth grader. She is in her sixth grade Sunday school class and is a full participant in the class and her church. In fact, today is her turn to acolyte. Leslie has a few friends in her Sunday school class who are also in her elementary school.

Leslie was born blind. It is important to show the students how a person can be blind and be accepted into a sighted environment. The scripture in the story will be the same for this class session, Ephesians 4:1-16.

Leslie will:
1. Participate in her Sunday school class. We will talk about her white cane for mobility, use of Braille, and her education.

2. Acolyte. Introduce by asking, "How do you think Leslie will light and extinguish the candles?" After children give ideas, read the section. Effectiveness will increase if you have a child who has served as an acolyte in your class.

3. Go to the front of the sanctuary independently during the children's sermon.

4. At home, help prepare lunch, wash the dishes afterwards, and do her homework. Introduce by asking, "How does Leslie do her homework?"

5. Attend a Sunday school class function. Leslie is picked up for her Sunday school class's church grounds clean-up and pizza party. This section affords an opportunity to talk about attitudes of adults when interacting with a blind person. Read this section and stop before the conversation with the waitress. Ask the class how they might respond if they were a) Leslie, b) the teacher, or c) a classmate. It is important to stress that Leslie is both a child and a Christian. She should not be disrespectful to an adult, yet it is important to educate the waitress in responding to a blind person. After eliciting ideas from the students, finish reading the section.

6. Upon returning home, get ready for bed, have a quiet time (Braille Bible), say her prayers, and go to sleep.

Leslie Gilson

Leslie Gilson woke up, checked her watch, and realized that she had time to get ready for church and that today was her turn to acolyte.

"Morning," Leslie said as she walked into the kitchen and gave her mother and father a hug.

"Good morning, Sweetie," her father said. "You look very nice. Doesn't she, dear?"

"Yes, you do," replied her mother. "You always look nice. Remember that you are acolyting today, and going to your class's work day and pizza party this afternoon."

"I have my work clothes out, and the party will be fun!"

David, Leslie's fifteen-year-old brother, smiled at her and said, "And while you guys are sweating in the yard, the youth will be putting together a tutorial program for kids at the homeless shelter. Aren't you going to Romilio's for pizza? That's the best in town!"

"When you're a great group of eleven-year-olds doing God's work, what do you expect?" laughed Leslie.

The family finished eating and piled into the car to go to church. They attend Hope United Methodist Church, where Leslie is in the sixth grade class and David is in the high school class.

Leslie walks with a long white cane. When she was learning how to walk, her parents gave her a tiny baby cane so that she would have more confidence. As she grew, she was given canes to match her height. When she entered kindergarten, she was given mobility instruction by the school corporation so she could learn to use her cane to go anywhere she wished.

Leslie was born blind. At first her family and friends at church were very sad. But her parents knew that with God's help and the love of church friends, it would be okay. The Gilsons said that Leslie was to be treated like any other child. She always attended Sunday school, junior church, and vacation Bible school; books had to be tape recorded in advance for her. When she went into the sixth grade class and wanted to become an acolyte, she was taught the skills she needed.

"Leslie, wait up!" It was Leslie's friend Sara, who was Leslie's classmate in school and Sunday school.

"Hi, Sara. How did you do on today's lesson?"

"Okay, I guess. I think it's cool that we're all part of the body of Christ, even though we're all different," Sara said.

21

Session 3

The two friends arrived in their classroom. Their teacher, Mr. Dinsmore, who also had taught them as fifth graders, was about to open the session with prayer.

Leslie's Sunday school lessons are tape recorded for her. She has a Braille Bible, which comes in eighteen volumes. Because of its size, Leslie brings only the volume she needs for the lesson for the day.

Leslie is acolyting today. (*Ask students, "How do you think she acolytes, since she is blind?"*)

Leslie leaves class early so she can put on her acolyte's robe.

When the organ music begins, Leslie takes her cane in her right hand and the lighter in her left. She walks down the aisle, climbs the stairs to the altar, and puts her cane on the floor in front of her. In order to find the wick, she runs her hand up the candle until she touches the top, puts her finger away and lights the candle. She repeats the process for the other candle. Leslie picks up her cane, walks down the steps, and takes her seat.

As the service begins, Leslie reaches for her hymnal. She loves to sing and can't wait until she can join the choir. (*Ask the students, "How do you think Leslie is able to sing hymns?"*) Leslie has a Braille hymnal, which takes seven volumes.

One of Leslie's favorite parts of the service is the children's sermon. Leslie has been going to the front of the church for "their" sermon ever since she could remember. When she was little, she held David's hand. Now that she is eleven, she walks up on her own. In Leslie's church a different member of the congregation preaches the children's sermon each Sunday. Today is Mrs. Stevens' turn.

"What," Mrs. Stevens asked, "am I holding?" She let the children look and gave it to Leslie to feel.

"It looks like gears," Dennis stated.

Mrs. Stevens said, "It's the inside of a watch. There are many of these inside a watch or clock. How do you think we as a church and as Christians are like the inside of a watch?"

"We all work together!" "Each part is important!" "We depend on one another!" The group was enthusiastic that morning, and they had a good discussion with Mrs. Stevens.

After the service, it was Leslie's task to put out the candles and carry the light from the sanctuary. (*Ask the class, "How do you think Leslie puts out the candles?"*)

Leslie takes her cane in her right hand and the lighter in her left. When she reaches the altar, she puts her cane down, finds the left candle and snuffs it out with the bell. She moves to the right candle. The lighter must be relit, so she finds the top of the candle with her free hand, lights the lighter, snuffs out the right candle, picks up her cane, and walks up the aisle out of the sanctuary.

"Leslie," Mr. Dinsmore said after church, "I'll be picking up the kids starting around 3:30, so be outside waiting at 4:00."

"Okay, I'll see you then."

Leslie and her family returned home where they all helped prepare lunch. Mr. and Mrs. Gilson peeled and cleaned the vegetables, David and Leslie sliced the cold meat and cheese to go in the salad.

"Mom," asked Leslie, "after lunch, will you read my history lesson to me?"

"Sure, and while we are on the subject of school, how is your research project on earthquakes coming?"

"Fine. I was able to find some books at the library and Mrs. Johnson read them to me. Now I have to start writing the paper."

After lunch, Leslie washed the dishes while David dried them and put them away.

When Leslie started school, she attended classes for Braille, mobility instruction for white cane, and keyboarding. Now that she has these skills, she spends most of her school time with her sixth grade class. Many of her textbooks are on tape, which she reads on a machine from her state library for the blind. Leslie's parents, David, and some people from church, like Mrs. Johnson, read books that are not on tape or in Braille. Leslie has a computer that has speech output which allows her to write her papers independently.

After lunch, Leslie began writing her paper on earthquakes, then her mother read the history lesson to her, and she began reading a Braille book on Michelangelo. Before she knew it, it was 4:00.

"Mom, Dad, I'm heading out. Mr. Dinsmore will be here any minute."

"I know it's Mr. Dinsmore's treat, Leslie, but here is five dollars," Mr. Gilson said.

(Ask the class, "How do you think Leslie tells the difference between different denominations of paper money?")

Leslie thanked her father, folded the bill in half, and put it in her wallet. She had developed special ways of folding her money so that she could keep track of the paper money easily. Coins were no problem for her because of their different sizes, weights, and the difference in their edges. Leslie

Session 3

had been interested to hear that the second place winner in the 1995 Westinghouse Awards for young scientists was a seventeen-year-old woman who had made a wallet-sized "bill reader" which would announce in its computer voice what kind of money was inserted in it. She hoped the young woman would be successful in getting her invention to market soon.

"Have fun, and remember, not everybody understands that it's all right to be blind," warned Mrs. Gilson.

"I'll be okay. Bye!"

Leslie didn't have to wait long. Mr. Dinsmore pulled up in his van a few minutes after Leslie left the house. He had already picked up Sara, Michael, Ellen, Joe, and Adam. Mrs. Dinsmore, a teacher at Leslie's school, was in the passenger seat. "Hi, Leslie," Mrs. Dinsmore said. "Just climb in next to Ellen."

The Gilsons live closest to the church, so Leslie was the last one to be picked up.

Mr. Dinsmore explained, "When we get to the church, I will split you into work groups and you can pick the job you want to do."

Joe groaned, "Aw, Mr. D, can't we skip the work and just go for the pizza?"

"Sorry, work first."

They arrived at the church and piled out of the van.

Mr. Dinsmore got them together and said, "First, vinyl gloves for everybody. I have two jobs that you may select from: picking up cans, bottles, and paper or raking the yard."

Leslie was teamed with Michael and Ellen. Their group chose to rake the yard. She raked a small area, picked up what she raked, put it in a cardboard box, and went to the next spot. When Leslie was finished, she called, "Michael, have I got everything?"

Michael walked over to her. "You missed a few leaves to your left, otherwise, it's clean."

"Thanks."

Leslie knelt, looked for the leaves and put them in the box. The clean-up took about an hour. The class was hot, dirty, and hungry.

"Okay, group," Mr. Dinsmore said. "Good work! Now let's wash up and go for pizza!"

24

Everyone cheered.

The group arrived at Romilio's and took a big table in the corner of the room. The waitress arrived to take their pizza, beverage, and appetizer order. The thirsty kids ordered two pitchers of pop immediately, and each one ordered an appetizer.

When the waitress came to Leslie, she asked Mr. Dinsmore, "And what would the little b-l-i-n-d girl like?"

(*At this point, ask the class, "What would you do if you were Leslie, and someone acted in this manner?" Solicit ideas, then read on.*)

"I will have the breaded zucchini sticks," Leslie said.

"Boy, what a doof!" Adam said, after the waitress had gone.

"Let's not be too critical. She probably doesn't know how to respond to a blind person," Mr. Dinsmore stated.

Sara said, "Ellen and Les, do you want to play a few CD's on the juke box?"

"Sure."

The three friends got up and walked over to the juke box. Leslie carried her cane in one hand and took Ellen's right arm in the other.

(*Explain to the class that Leslie will be a half-step behind Ellen and will know what is in front of her by using her cane.*)

They selected the songs they wanted to hear and retuned to the table. The waitress brought their appetizer and pop orders a few minutes later.

"Excuse me, sir, but can the blind girl feed herself?" the waitress asked Mr. Dinsmore.

(*Ask the class, "How could you respond to the waitress's question if you were a) Mr. Dinsmore, b) Leslie, or c) her classmates?"*)

"Yes, ma'am, Leslie can feed herself," Mr. Dinsmore said.

"Miss, I don't mean to be disrespectful," Leslie told the waitress, "I'm only blind. My eyes may not work, but my brain does. I can do anything that my friends at this table do." The waitress smiled and walked away.

There were whispers of "Way to go, Les!" Mr. Dinsmore had to tell them to be quiet. The pizza came a few minutes later and the kids ate, talked, and laughed through the meal. Leslie arrived home at 7:30.

"Hi!" David said. "Did you have a good time?"

"Yes, I did. The pizza was great and the church yard is clean."

"We were waiting for you to get home," Mrs. Gilson said. "We were going to watch the described version of *Beethoven*."

(*Described Video Service describes action, scenery, and facial expressions of movies without interfering with the story of the movie. Leslie receives movies from her state Library for the Blind.*)

"Great," Leslie said, and settled down to watch the movie.

After *Beethoven* was over, Leslie kissed her parents and David goodnight, then went upstairs to get ready for bed. She took her shower and brushed her teeth. In her room, Leslie laid out her clothes and books for school. She took a volume of her Braille Bible, read the day's scriptures, and thought about what she had read before she said her prayers.

"Yes," Leslie thought as she settled into bed, "it is good to be a child of God."

DISCUSSION:
Use the questions listed in the introductory material or in the body of the story to discuss various aspects of Leslie's story. Encourage the class to think of how they might respond to Leslie if she were in their own Sunday school class.

BIBLE STUDY:
Read Ephesians 4:1-16 together. Ask the students to look at parts of their own bodies and think of the marvelous things they do. Explain that in the church we are like parts of a whole body, each with our own jobs to do and our own gifts to bring.

CLOSING:
Close with prayer for our various gifts, and pray for insight into ways we can accept and encourage the gifts of others.

Session 4
Understanding Physical Handicaps
by Timothy A. Powers

PURPOSE:
Children will learn about various physical handicaps and will become more sensitive to those persons who are physically handicapped.

MATERIALS:
>Two or three wheelchairs
>Construction cones
>One or two wooden ramps (if possible)
>Newsprint or chalkboard
>Copies of the word search sheet, *What Helps Make Lives Easier?*
>Pencils or pens
>Bibles

SUGGESTION:
Many people within your community may have had occasion to use wheelchairs, walkers, canes, or braces at one time, and may be willing to lend them to you. Local hospitals or nursing homes may also be a source of equipment. Persons with handicapping conditions may be delighted to help you construct a course that would help your class understand their experiences more clearly.

OPENING ACTIVITY:
WHEELCHAIR OBSTACLE COURSE (Five to ten minutes)
Greet the children as they come in. Tell them you're going to begin by playing a game. If possible go outside or have them move to a large indoor area where you have set up an obstacle course using construction cones, ramps, and, if possible, different kinds of surfaces.

Have two or three wheelchairs available. Say, *"We're going to see how things we take for granted can be very difficult for some people. We can walk around different obstacles, but some people can't. So we're going to see how hard it can be for some people to get around."*

Then have them take turns trying to maneuver the wheelchairs through the obstacle course. This can be done in one of two ways. The children can either take themselves through it or they can take turns riding and pushing. Have them switch positions after a few minutes. Explain this is NOT a race but a way to see how difficult certain barriers can be. (Note: If you can go outside, make use of the barriers that may exist in your church's parking lot.)

DISCUSSION: (Five minutes)
Bring the class back together and return to your room if you left it. Ask, *"How did it feel to be in the wheelchair and try to get around those obstacles? What did it feel like to have someone push you? What did it feel like to push someone in a wheelchair? How could we make it easier for someone in a wheelchair to get around?"*

27

WHAT ARE PHYSICAL HANDICAPS? (Five minutes)

Say, *"There are all kinds of reasons why a person could be in a wheelchair. There are also people who walk with crutches, canes, or walkers, or who have braces on their legs. There are people missing arms or legs. These are all called physical handicaps. That means that something about their bodies makes it difficult to do things that most people take for granted."*

On a sheet of newsprint or a chalkboard ask the children to name some physical handicaps. Explain a little about each one. Some possible answers are:

Cerebral Palsy — A condition caused by brain damage due to lack of oxygen or a blow to the head either before or shortly after birth. It causes certain muscles to be hard to control.

Paraplegic — Paralysis of the legs usually caused by spinal injury.

Quadriplegic — Paralysis affecting the arms and legs, again usually caused by spinal injury.

Amputee — Having one or more limbs removed by surgery or being born without one or more limbs.

WORD SEARCH: (Ten minutes)

Pass out copies of the word search page. Pass out pencils or pens if needed. Give the class ten minutes to find the words. Explain that each of the hidden words is something that helps make life easier for people with handicaps.

THE BIBLE: (Ten minutes)

Genesis 1:26-27

Read this passage. Write on newsprint or chalkboard: THE IMAGE OF GOD.

Ask, *"What does it mean to be created in the image of God?"* You might mention after hearing some answers that it doesn't mean we look LIKE God, but that we are SPECIAL in God's sight. That includes physically handicapped people. Ask, *"What can we do to help others feel special and loved by God, especially what can we do to help those who are physically handicapped?"*

CLOSING: (Five minutes)

Gather the class in a circle and pray, thanking God for making each person special. Thank God for those who try to make life easier for persons with physical handicaps. Ask God to help make us all more sensitive to the needs of other people.

What Helps Make Lives Easier?

Can you find these words that help make life easier for persons with physical handicaps?

Ramps	Curb Cuts	Artificial Limbs
Braces	Elevator	Accessibility
Vans	Crutches	Wheelchair
Lifts	Parking	Walker

```
T  G  E  E  F  W  V  A  N  S  E  A
C  Y  T  W  S  L  I  F  T  S  S  D
U  S  P  M  A  R  I  L  R  A  V  Q
R  D  V  I  E  L  E  V  A  T  O  R
B  W  S  G  N  I  K  R  A  P  A  C
C  H  S  T  H  N  I  E  C  G  S  R
U  E  B  W  F  G  N  I  R  X  E  U
T  E  M  E  W  S  P  Y  B  D  J  T
S  L  I  C  Y  D  K  G  N  B  O  C
Z  C  L  F  G  T  D  S  C  Q  I  H
Y  H  L  Y  D  F  V  N  Y  R  D  E
X  A  A  T  W  S  D  V  B  G  J  S
A  I  I  I  G  G  T  H  F  T  U  M
I  R  C  L  O  P  G  T  H  J  K  F
S  W  I  I  I  Y  T  H  G  J  K  L
W  B  F  B  R  A  C  E  S  M  G  D
S  X  I  I  G  B  N  H  J  K  L  Y
E  W  T  S  H  G  F  R  T  I  O  D
B  N  R  S  K  L  F  D  S  A  W  E
O  I  A  E  H  J  K  L  G  B  H  F
S  E  D  C  R  T  Y  U  I  L  H  N
W  R  T  C  F  S  R  T  Y  U  I  O
S  A  E  A  R  T  Y  U  I  O  P  G
```

29

Key

What Helps Make Lives Easier?

Can you find these words that help make life eaiser for persons with physical handicaps?

Ramps	Curb Cuts	Artificial Limbs
Braces	Elevator	Accessibility
Vans	Crutches	Wheelchair
Lifts	Parking	Walker

```
T  G  E  E  F  W  V  A  N  S  E  A
C  Y  T  W  S  L  I  F  T  S  S  D
U  S  P  M  A  R  I  L  R  A  V  Q
R  D  V  I  E  L  E  V  A  T  O  R
B  W  S  G  N  I  K  R  A  P  A  C
C  H  S  T  H  N  I  E  C  G  S  R
U  E  B  W  F  G  N  I  R  X  E  U
T  E  M  E  W  S  P  Y  B  D  J  T
S  L  I  C  Y  D  K  G  N  B  O  C
Z  C  L  F  G  T  D  S  C  Q  I  H
Y  H  L  Y  D  F  V  N  Y  R  D  E
X  A  A  T  W  S  D  V  B  G  J  S
A  I  I  I  G  G  T  H  F  T  U  M
I  R  C  L  O  P  G  T  H  J  K  F
S  W  I  I  I  Y  T  H  G  J  K  L
W  B  F  B  R  A  C  E  S  M  G  D
S  W  I  I  G  B  N  H  J  K  L  Y
E  W  T  S  H  G  F  R  T  I  O  D
B  N  R  S  K  L  F  D  S  A  W  E
O  I  A  E  H  J  K  L  G  B  H  F
S  E  D  C  R  T  Y  U  I  L  H  N
W  R  T  C  F  S  R  T  Y  U  I  O
S  A  E  A  R  T  Y  U  I  O  P  G
```

30

Session 5
Understanding Physical Handicaps II
by Timothy A. Powers

PURPOSE:
Children will learn ways we, as a church, can help people with physical handicaps feel welcome and learn that all people are created in the image of God.

MATERIALS NEEDED:

> Enough large shirts to go around the class
> Newsprint or chalkboard
> Bibles
> Paper and pencils, pens, or crayons
> Copies of *Feelings* word search for each student

OPENING ACTIVITY:
ONE-HANDED DAY (Ten minutes)
Greet the children as they come in. Have a pile of large shirts in the center of the room (one for each child). Say, *"Last week we started talking about physical handicaps. We had an obstacle course to show how hard it can be for some people to get around. This week we're going to look at how hard it can be for some people to do even simple things like get dressed. Many people lose the use of one of their hands because of accidents or by birth, or by a stroke. We're going to see how they would start their day."*

Have all children pick out a shirt and untie or loosen their shoes. Tell them they have to put the shirt on and fasten their shoes by only using their good hand. (NOTE: You may want to have them hold up the hand they normally use for most things first.) The shirts must be put on and buttoned by only using their one hand. This is not a race; we are trying to see how difficult some activities can be.

DISCUSSION: (Five minutes)
Bring the class back together and ask, *"How did it feel trying to get dressed using only one hand? Was it hard or easy? Did you feel like asking for help? Why didn't you? Would a person with only one hand need help? Did you find a new way to button your shirt or tie your shoes?"*

ROLE-PLAY AND DISCUSSION: (Ten minutes)
Say, *"Now we're going to pretend in two different situations. Both of them involve handicapped people. We're going to see what it might feel like if we were physically handicapped and these two things happened."*

1. The Car In The Parking Space
Pick two of the children. One will be a person in a wheelchair driving a van; the other will be a person in a car. The van arrives at the supermarket, only to find a person parking his or her car in the space reserved for handicapped persons. The person in the car should be very rude to the person in the van. Watch and see what happens.

After a few minutes of role-playing, ask, *"How did you feel as the physically handicapped person when the car was in your space? How did you feel as the person in the car?"* (To the class) *"What would you do if you saw someone parking in a handicapped space who doesn't need to be there?"*

Show the class the handicapped symbol and remind them that those spaces marked with this symbol are only for people who need to park there.

2. A Visitor At Church

Pick five or six different children. One will be a person with a physical handicap; the others will be various people in a church or Sunday school class. The person with the handicap is visiting this Sunday, and the others in the church are trying to make him or her feel comfortable and welcome. Have them role play for a few minutes about how they would do that. After the role-play ask, *"How did you feel as a visitor? Welcome or unwelcome? How did it feel to try to make someone with a physical handicap welcome? What could we do as a church or Sunday school class to help people feel welcome?"*

HOW ARE WE DOING AS A CHURCH? (Five minutes)

Pass out paper and pencils, pens, or crayons. Have the class draw or write ways our church could do more to make people with physical handicaps feel welcome. Share pictures or answers as a class and with the pastor, chairperson of the administrative board or council, or with the board of trustees.

THE BIBLE: (Ten minutes)

Mark 2:1-12

Read or retell the story of the paralytic being lowered down to meet Jesus.

Ask, *"How did the paralytic feel? What was going through the minds of the crowd? How did Jesus treat the paralytic? What can we learn about how we should treat physically handicapped people?"*

2 Corinthians 12:7-10

Read this scripture. Say, *"We read a lot about Jesus healing people. But sometimes physical healing doesn't come. When it doesn't happen, we need to trust in God's love for all people. God's strength is shown in our weakness. How? Trust in God is necessary on our part. We may not always understand God's plans, but we know that God always acts in our best interest."*

WORD SEARCH: (Five minutes)

Pass out the word search sheets and have each child look for these ideas which were present in the scripture passage from Mark.

CLOSING: (Five minutes)

Gather in a circle and pray for God's blessing on all the children in the class. Ask God to help the class help others to know they are special, and loved by God.

Feelings

Handicapped   All   Loves
Wheelchair   Lame   Jesus
Sensitive   Bible   Feelings
Paralyzed

```
M  T  B  O  O  P  G  I  G  A  U  O
Q  J  P  A  R  A  L  Y  Z  E  D  D
U  R  I  A  H  C  L  E  E  H  W  Y
H  A  N  D  I  C  A  P  P  E  D  R
I  M  E  L  P  B  Z  E  D  A  R  E
M  C  V  N  N  C  S  E  V  O  L  O
B  N  I  M  S  G  N  I  L  E  E  F
B  W  T  J  X  Z  E  S  U  S  E  J
M  F  I  A  T  O  X  L  B  N  M  H
N  O  S  L  L  I  F  Z  B  R  W  V
D  Y  N  L  C  F  M  N  Y  I  V  Q
D  O  E  I  X  D  W  J  V  A  B  I
O  U  S  R  L  A  M  E  R  N  M  M
```

Key

Feelings

Handicapped	All	Loves
Wheelchair	Lame	Jesus
Sensitive	Bible	Feelings
Paralyzed		

```
M   T   B   O   O   P   G   I   G   A   U   O
Q   J   P   A   R   A   L   Y   Z   E   D   D
U   R   I   A   H   C   L   E   E   H   W   Y
H   A   N   D   I   C   A   P   P   E   D   R
I   M   E   L   P   B   Z   E   D   A   R   E
M   C   V   N   N   C   S   E   V   O   L   O
B   N   I   M   S   G   N   I   L   E   E   F
B   W   T   J   X   Z   E   S   U   S   E   J
M   F   I   A   T   O   X   L   B   N   M   H
N   O   S   L   L   I   F   Z   B   R   W   V
D   Y   N   L   C   F   M   N   Y   I   V   Q
D   O   E   I   X   D   W   J   V   A   B   I
O   U   S   R   L   A   M   E   R   N   M   M
```

34

Session 6
Deafness And Hearing Impairment
by Joe Smith

Over 24 million people in America, half of them under 65 years of age, are afflicted with hearing loss. They also experience difficulties in communication, have feelings of low self-esteem or inadequacy, and may occasionally develop paranoid traits if they erroneously think that other persons are talking about them because they cannot hear what is being said in conversation.

Hearing impaired persons may also be seen as rude or inconsiderate if they interrupt a conversation to share their viewpoint without realizing that someone else is still speaking. They can become loners and seek to compensate for their auditory loss by development of visual and kinesthetic talents.

*Theologian Daniel Day Williams in **The Minister and the Care of Souls** writes that "in the New Testament faith as in the Old, the language of salvation and the language of healing are interwoven." An aim of Christian education is to impart this spirit of healing and reconciliation. With hearing impaired persons specifically, it is to help them realize that the problem lies with their hearing and not with them.*

PURPOSE:
1. To experience to some degree what hearing loss is like.
2. To learn that Jesus desires salvation and healing for all persons.
3. To increase sensitivity to and compassion for those afflicted with hearing loss.

MATERIALS NEEDED:
> Cotton or ear plugs for each class member
> Pens, pencils, or crayons and paper
> Copies of the *Jesus Heals A Deaf-Mute* Bible worksheet for each child

OPTIONAL ACTIVITY:
Invite a person who is hearing impaired or deaf to address the class this week or next, sharing experiences from his/her own life. Some people will know and use American Sign Language, and this makes an interesting demonstration. Others will use lip reading or various adaptive technologies.

ACTIVITIES:
1. Provide cotton or ear plugs for the students in your class. Have them try to copy a sentence or two that you read to them. Have them pair off and try to carry on a conversation with each other. Students will notice that sound will be hollow or muffled. They may pick up parts of the conversation but not all of it. They may be frustrated. After the exercise have the class talk about their feelings and what it was like for them.

2. Read Mark 7:31-37 from *Today's English Version* or a Bible translation for children. This is the passage from which the title of this whole curriculum is taken (see Introduction). Have the children put the story in their own words. Ask them why a person who has difficulty hearing might have trouble with speech. What do they learn about Jesus from this story? *Emphasize that "dumbness," found in some translations, has nothing to do with one's intelligence.*

3. Have students share their own personal experiences. Perhaps a student is hearing impaired or has a family member or friend who is. Students can share their experiences. Children can be fascinated by someone who wears a hearing aid who comes in and demonstrates what it is like and how it works or by someone who knows American Sign Language and can teach them a phrase or a song.

4. Have children look at their church to see what ministries are offered to enhance the hearing of all persons. Does someone sign? Are loop or infrared microphone systems available? What about acoustical tile or various means to reduce echoes? What about the importance of seeing the lips of a speaker when that person is talking?

5. Discuss how it feels to be different in any aspect when you are trying to fit in and just be like anybody else. What can the students do by way of words or actions to help people be accepted and part of the group? What would Jesus have us do?

6. Let students fill in the blanks on the Bible worksheet provided.

CLOSING:
End with a prayer of thanksgiving for God's gift of adaptability that allows those who are deaf or hard of hearing to create ingenious ways of living in the world. Pray for sensitivity and openness on the part of those who are hearing, that they may be open to the needs of all.

Jesus Heals A Deaf-Mute

Mark 7:31-37 — *The Good News Bible (Today's English Version)*

³¹ Jesus then left the _____ of _____ and went on through _____ to Lake _____, going by way of the territory of the _____ Towns. ³² Some people brought him a man who was _____ and could hardly _____, and they begged _____ to place his _____ on him. ³³ So Jesus took him off _____, away from the _____, put his _____ in the man's _____, _____, and touched the man's _____. ³⁴ Then Jesus looked up to _____, gave a deep _____, and said to the man, "_____," which means, "_____!"

³⁵ At once the man was able to _____, his _____ impediment was removed, and he began to _____ without any trouble. ³⁶ Then Jesus ordered the people not to _____ of it to any one; but the more he ordered them not to, the more they _____ it. ³⁷ And all who heard were completely _____. "How well he does everything!" they exclaimed. "He even causes the _____ to _____ and the _____ to _____!"

Session 6

Key

Jesus Heals A Deaf-Mute

Mark 7:31-37 — *The Good News Bible* (Today's English Version)

31 Jesus then left the __neighborhood__ of __Tyre__ and went on through __Sidon__ to Lake __Galilee__, going by way of the territory of the __Ten__ Towns. 32 Some people brought him a man who was __deaf__ and could hardly __speak__, and they begged __Jesus__ to place his __hands__ on him. 33 So Jesus took him off __alone__, away from the __crowd__, put his __fingers__ in the man's __ears__, __spat__, and touched the man's __tongue__. 34 Then Jesus looked up to __heaven__, gave a deep __groan__, and said to the man, "__Ephphatha__," which means, "__Open up__!"

35 At once the man was able to __hear__, his __speech__ impediment was removed, and he began to __talk__ without any trouble. 36 Then Jesus ordered the people not to __speak__ of it to any one; but the more he ordered them not to, the more they __told__ it. 37 And all who heard were completely __amazed__. "How well he does everything!" they exclaimed. "He even causes the __deaf__ to __hear__ and the __dumb__ to __speak__!"

Session 7
Communication
by Sherrie Drake

PURPOSE:

1. To build on last week's discussion about deafness and hearing impairment by exploring how difficult communication can be for *everyone* at times.

2. To discover that there are many different methods of communicating, that verbal communication is only part of the picture.

MATERIALS NEEDED:

A "Once Upon A A Time" Sign (see *Activity #1*)
Children's building blocks or geometric shapes cut from construction paper
(see *Activity #2*)
"Feeling Cards" (see *Activity #3*)

ACTIVITIES:

1. How Hard Is It To ReallySee?

Cut a triangle from poster board with equal sides, each at least 12" long. Print in magic marker the following words, arranging them in the triangle as shown below:

Tell the class you are going to hold up a sign for them to read, and ask them to call out what is written on it as soon as they see what it is. Chances are very good that they will call out, "Once upon a time," and never even notice that you have repeated the word "A" two times. Through discussion, point out that most of the time we see things the way we *think* they should be, not always the way they actually *are*. Explain that this makes communication difficult, because two people can think they are talking clearly to one another, yet mistakes and misunderstandings happen easily. Ask if anyone in the class can think of an example of a misunderstanding that has happened to them, maybe in the past week. Examples could include such things as a mom or dad who picks them up at the wrong time for a school activity, a chore or job that they were expected to do at home that they didn't understand was their responsibility, or a "date" set between friends to meet at a particular location on the playground that didn't materialize. Explain that today's session is going to focus on paying attention to ways we communicate with each other.

2. How Hard Is It To Listen?

Choose two volunteers to sit down, back to back on the floor. (If your class is very large, you may wish to have two or more pairs doing this activity simultaneously.) Allow the rest of the class to stand in a circle and watch, but caution them that they will *not* be allowed to speak during the activity.

Place in front of each volunteer a collection of fifteen to twenty children's books of differing sizes and shapes. Make sure, however, that each volunteer gets the same grouping, such as six rectangles, four squares, an arch, four columns, three small triangles, and two long ramps apiece. The color of the blocks does not matter. This activity can also be done with an arrangement of geometric shapes cut from construction paper, if no blocks are available.

Instruct one of the partners to take a couple of minutes to build something out of his or her blocks. Explain that it can be anything — a shape, a tower, a design on the floor; let them feel free to use their imaginations.

When they are done, explain that now their task is to tell their partner how to build the exact same formation they have built. They may speak to each other, the partner may ask any kind of question(s) he or she wishes to, but they may *not* look at one another or at the other's creation during the process. The original builder will have to rely on the partner's verbal descriptions alone to gauge how well his or her partner is understanding the instructions he or she is giving. You will probably need to continually remind the "instruction giver" not to turn around and peek, because the temptation to do this is *very* strong.

When the first team has finished, allow others to try the same activity.

Afterwards, have a discussion about what happened. Find out where there were frustrations, and who preferred giving the instructions and who preferred receiving them. Ask those who had watched a few "rounds" whether that experience made it easier for them when it was their turn to try. Notice if anyone points out how much he or she relies on senses other than hearing for communication.

3. What Can Faces Show?

Ask for a volunteer who would be willing to act out something in front of the class. Have prepared a box or coffee can containing "Feeling Cards" — small slips of paper or index cards with a single emotion word written on each one.

Tell your volunteer privately that he or she is to reach into the container, pull out a card, then try to get the class to guess what the feeling is by using only the expression on his or her face. If they cannot guess within a reasonable time, allow the actor to use his or her whole body and movements, but do not allow them to speak or make verbal noises.

Prepare the class by announcing that your volunteer is going to, at your signal, show a feeling, and ask the class to shout out their guesses about what the feeling is as soon as they see it.

Feelings for the cards could include [but not be limited to] mad, sad, happy, worried, scared, excited, and puzzled. You may also decide to use degrees of emotion — ecstatic vs. happy, for example.

After the activity discuss how it was that people could guess what the actor was feeling, even though he or she didn't use words. Ask if it was (or would be) easier to guess when the person used his or her whole body. Ask the actor(s) about their experience trying to communicate feelings without using words.

4. Bible Study
Divide the class into four groups, and have them look up the following passages, preferably using a Bible for children, or a translation such as the *Good News Bible*, which is easy for children to read:
> Genesis 12:1-3
> Exodus 13:20-22
> Luke 1:26-33
> John 11:25-26

When everyone has found his assigned passage, explain that God has many different ways of communicating with people in the Bible. Sometimes God uses a sign or a miracle. Sometimes God speaks directly to people. Sometimes God uses a messenger, such as an angel. And in Jesus, God came to communicate with his whole life. Ask each group to give their idea of how God is communicating with people in the passage they read. Ask one volunteer from each group to read his passage aloud, so that the entire class can participate in the discussion.

Discuss whether God still communicates with us today, and be prepared to suggest ways in which this happens if they are having difficulty coming up with ideas. (You may want to point out that part of what the church does in the world is hold up ways God communicates with us through the use of scripture, baptism, communion, the witness of believers, prayer, and so forth.)

CLOSING:
Form a circle for prayer. Explain that all of us have difficulty communicating with others from time to time. This can be especially annoying when we feel like we're trying our best to get along with moms, dads, grandparents, brothers, sisters, friends, teachers, coaches, and others, but things just don't go quite as we would like. Announce that you are going to give a moment of quiet time, and you would like each person to think of one other person with whom they'd like to communicate more clearly. Then give time for anyone who wishes to speak the name of the person they have in mind out loud, to be held up in prayer.

Close by praying for any situations that have been mentioned, and by praying that we would continue to be sensitive to the ways God communicates with us in our lives.

Session 8
"Slow" And "Stupid" Are *Not* The Same
by Betty Stewart

PURPOSE:
To help create, develop, and encourage in young people an awareness of and sensitivity toward children with developmental disabilities.

MATERIALS:
> List of instructions for first activity
> Video: *Jesus' Bicycle*, available from North Indiana Conference Media Resource Library. There is no rental fee, churches pay shipping and handling only.

BACKGROUND INFORMATION:
When talking about any form of retardation, some children may ask "why?" or how someone "gets like that." We know accidents happen, some children are abused, and some people are born with a problem.

Sometimes part of the brain does not develop as it should. Fluid fills the area which should have contained brain tissue. This causes children to be slow in speech and motor development.

Some children don't hear well, or not at all. Some children who are born this way or have been in an accident will never walk or run. Others might walk but with difficulty.

However, love is there. Most children who have a handicap are very loving and respond well to kindness. They are special children and need to know they are loved.

EXPANDING THE SESSION:
In addition to these materials, you may want to arrange a field trip with your class to a local group home or sheltered workshop.

PROCEDURE:
Discussion:
Following an opening prayer, begin the session with questions.
> 1. Do you have a friend, brother, sister, cousin who is different?
> 2. How do you feel when you are around that person (or think you might feel)?
> 3. Do your friends, parents, or other adults treat you in a different way when they are with someone who has a disability?
> 4. How does this make you feel? Angry? Hurt? Lonely? Happy? Close discussion by suggesting reasons adults might treat a child with a disability differently, e.g. fear, frustration, hurt, hostility, puzzlement, and so on.

Activity 1:

With many forms of retardation people are perfectly capable of understanding directions, carrying on conversations, working, reading, and writing; it's just that they need more time to process the information they're given. It can be terribly frustrating to feel overwhelmed by the barrage of sights, words, ideas, and sounds which our world throws at us each day. Teachers of children with these special needs sometimes need to do nothing more than slow way down when giving instructions, allowing the class time to process one idea before moving on to the next.

In an effort to help your class glimpse some of the frustration slower thinkers may experience, prepare two lists of instructions for simple activities they can do in the classroom. Ideas include: "stand up," "turn around twice," "walk to the blackboard and back," "stick out your tongue," "hop on one foot," "touch your nose with your right hand," "pretend to comb your hair," "bend over and touch your toes," and so on.

Have about ten items on each list. The activities on the two lists may overlap, but the order should be different from one list to the next.

Have your class follow the instructions on the first list. Read at a pace that is comfortable, allowing plenty of time for kids to act on one instruction before moving to the next.

Tell the class that you're going to do the activity again, but this time be prepared to read the second list of instructions very quickly, allowing no time between the lists for the children to act.

When you've finished the second list, sit with the kids and discuss what it felt like, trying to follow instructions both times. They may have felt frustrated, confused, even slightly angry the second time through.

Video:

Watch *Jesus' Bicycle*, a 21-minute video dealing with mental retardation. Follow with discussion, questions, and answers.

Jesus' Bicycle is the story of two very special children — six-year-old Emily and Dirk, who is a young man with both mental and physical disabilities.

After Emily's mother reads her a story based on Jesus' love for children, Emily is left with lots of time to play and explore before dinner. Her curiosity carries her farther and farther away from home, along the streets of her neighborhood and into the heart of town. Soon, she becomes lost and begins to be frightened. Emily's ultimate faith in a nurturing world is affirmed when Dirk, alerted by Emily's worried mother, comes to rescue Emily on his very special bike. Together, Emily and Dirk brave a dramatic adventure, highlighted by an exciting chase as they are pursued by some cruel neighborhood boys while they try to make their way back home. This beautiful and touching presentation teaches us to look for Christ in all those around us. *Leaders guide included.*

CLOSING:

Ask the class to imagine that they have a disability, or to imagine someone close to them who has a disability. Then ask them to suggest ways they would like to be treated. Make a list of words on the board that describe their answers. Ask if they think God would approve of these kind ways of acting.

Close with a prayer that God would open our hearts to gentle ways of treating one another.

Session 9
Kindness Is Always In Order
by Betty Stewart

PURPOSE:
1. To follow up on last week's thinking about how to treat someone with a handicapping condition.
2. To begin to consider that kindness is always in order, no matter who it is with whom we interact.

MATERIALS:
>Copy of *Kindness* word search for each student
>Copy of *Helping* connect the dots coloring sheet for each student
>Copy of *Random Acts of Kindness* checklist for each student
>Bibles
>Long sheet of butcher or shelf paper taped to wall for mural
>Markers or crayons for mural (check markers for "bleed through" first)

PROCEDURE:
Worksheets:
As children enter, have them work on *Kindness* word search and *Helping* connect the dots until the whole class has gathered.

Discussion:
Remind students of the list they generated last week of ways in which they would like to be treated if they had handicaps or if someone close to them was handicapped. Point out that these ways of behaving are really the ways we should be treating all people. Ask if anyone has a story he would like to share about a time when he was either treated rudely, making him feel unhappy, or when he was treated with respect, making him feel good and whole.

Class Mural:
Explain that the large sheet of blank paper on the wall is for a Kindness mural that everyone is going to work on. Have the children think of places they would be during a typical week (school, home, sports practice, shopping mall, grocery store, and so forth). On the mural block out space for three or four of the places they suggest. Assign groups to work on each one of these scenes, asking them to draw both the place and at least one example of something happening that shows kindness in the place they are drawing. For example, the "home" scene could show a house with a child helping his or her brother mow the lawn; the "grocery store" could have someone helping another person carry bags of groceries to her car, and so on.

When everyone has finished, have each group explain what they drew and tell what is happening in each scene.

If there is time at the end of class, allow the participants to return to the mural and draw "linking scenes" such as roads, automobiles, and background landscapes that will complete the mural as a whole.

Bible:
Use the following verses to track down clues about how God would have us behave toward one another. Have the class look up each passage. Ask someone who is comfortable reading aloud to read the verse(s). Then have the children explain what it says about kindness or ways to treat other people.

Nehemiah 9:15	Matthew 18:1-5	2 Corinthians 6:6
Proverbs 15:1	Luke 10:33-34	Galatians 3:28
Isaiah 61:1	1 Corinthians 12:26	Ephesians 4:32

CLOSING:
Distribute *Random Acts of Kindness* checklists for children to take home. Invite them to use the coming week as a time to practice these or other ways of being kind. Ask them to check off any of the activities which apply to them during the course of the week. Encourage them to bring their sheets to you next week to show you ways they have practiced being considerate of others.

Close with a prayer that God will help them put kindness into action in their lives, and that their action will make a difference to someone in the coming week.

Kindness

Kindness	Courteous	Manners
Good	Lend	Play
Clean	Carry	Help
Respect	Friends	People
Cheer	Tutor	Share
Work	Nice	Talk

```
C  V  U  X  V  B  Q  L  O  P  V  C
D  Y  P  Z  R  S  S  S  T  E  S  C
O  S  Z  K  S  U  E  G  A  O  K  L
O  Q  F  C  D  O  U  Q  X  P  D  K
G  X  B  N  N  E  R  H  Q  L  K  T
Q  R  N  X  E  T  E  E  D  E  Y  U
L  O  N  M  I  R  E  L  F  I  Q  J
Y  T  C  J  R  U  H  P  H  A  F  I
A  U  K  N  F  O  C  L  E  N  D  S
L  T  P  E  R  C  K  U  S  J  Z  C
P  R  E  S  P  E  C  T  S  Q  M  A
M  K  S  K  P  S  S  Q  E  C  L  R
G  S  R  H  A  B  R  T  N  C  B  R
F  Q  N  O  A  O  F  E  D  I  I  Y
I  T  A  Q  W  R  N  Y  N  A  R  N
Q  I  E  U  D  T  E  M  I  N  V  V
J  N  L  C  S  M  Z  T  K  L  A  T
N  W  C  L  C  T  M  Z  D  B  U  M
```

Key

Kindness

Kindness	Courteous	Manners
Good	Lend	Play
Clean	Carry	Help
Respect	Friends	People
Cheer	Tutor	Share
Work	Nice	Talk

```
C  V  U  X  V  B  Q  L  O  P  V  C
D  Y  P  Z  R  S  S  S  T  E  S  C
O  S  Z  K  S  U  E  G  A  O  K  L
O  Q  F  C  D  O  U  Q  X  P  D  K
G  X  B  N  N  E  R  H  Q  L  K  T
Q  R  N  X  E  T  E  E  D  E  Y  U
L  O  N  M  I  R  E  L  F  I  Q  J
Y  T  C  J  R  U  E  P  H  A  F  I
A  U  K  N  F  O  H  L  E  N  D  S
L  T  P  E  R  C  C  P  S  J  Z  C
P  R  E  S  P  E  C  T  S  Q  M  A
M  K  S  K  P  S  S  Q  E  C  L  R
G  S  R  H  A  B  R  T  N  C  B  R
F  Q  N  O  A  O  F  E  D  I  I  Y
I  T  A  Q  W  R  N  Y  N  A  R  N
Q  I  E  U  D  T  E  M  I  N  V  V
J  N  L  C  S  M  Z  T  K  L  A  T
N  W  C  L  C  T  M  Z  D  B  U  M
```

Helping Means Thinking Of Others

Go Dot to Dot and Color.

After doing this, make up your own list of acts of kindness. Could this class have a project called "Acts of Kindness"? Discuss.

Practice Random Acts Of Kindness

Practice "random acts of kindness." When you see a chance to be kind ... JUST DO IT. You'll like the good feeling you have when you do something just to be kind, with no reward expected.

❏ Say "Good morning" when you get on the bus.

❏ Say "Thank you" when you get off.

❏ Say "Please," "Thank you," "Good work," "Nice try," or "Congratulations."

❏ If someone does something wrong, say, "It's all right."

❏ Help others with their work if they are having trouble understanding it.

❏ Call someone by his/her first name.

❏ Make someone feel better when he or she is hurt or sad about something.

❏ Play with a new kid and help him make friends so he won't be lonely.

❏ Stand up for your classmates.

❏ Respect others' rights and property.

❏ Tell someone what she missed if she was absent.

❏ Be polite and listen when someone is telling you something.

❏ Hold doors for kids whose hands are full.

❏ Be quiet so others can concentrate.

❏ Make your bed without being told.

❏ Share your toys with others.

❏ Keep your stuff off the floor.

❏ Clean up after yourself in the bathroom and kitchen.

❏ Stop someone from teasing another person.

❏ Talk to others about their problems.

❏ Hold a younger kid's hand when walking to or from school.

❏ Refuse to talk about someone behind his back.

❏ Be on time so others don't have to wait.

Session 10
How Does It Feel? How Can We Help?
by Ralph Karstedt

PURPOSE:
To have students share in the feelings of those with disabilities and to discover ways of being helpful to them.

MATERIALS:
> Blindfold
> Ear plugs
> Wheelchair
> Copy of *The Least of These* Bible worksheet for each student

PROCEDURE:
1. Select three students who will be "blind," "deaf," or "crippled" for the morning. These students should be respectively blindfolded, given ear plugs, and placed in a wheelchair. They should attend worship with their limitations, if possible.

2. Begin the class session with time for general conversation and planning for coming activities. Do not especially encourage students to be helpful to the "handicapped" ones. Allow events to take their own course.

3. As weather and church facilities allow, take the class on a nature walk or on an errand to some far part of the building. The "handicapped" students may go along or be left behind in the room. Allow the class to make its own decision about this.

4. When the walk or errand is over, invite the "handicapped" to share their feelings. How did it feel for them to be led, carried up and down stairs, or be unable to hear everything being said?

5. Have the class suggest ways they could have been more helpful. List these ideas on the chalkboard and discuss them. Possible suggestions: A blind person prefers to take his guide's arm rather than be pushed. One who has hearing problems should be seated in the center of the class. He will be helped if key words are written on the chalkboard. One who is in a wheelchair may feel terribly insecure if carried up or down steps and very left out if not included in activities.

6. You may want to invite the pastor, Administrative Board chairperson, or trustee to participate in the class and join the discussion. With their help, you could list on the board ways in which your church is already open to and equipped for those with disabilities, and ways in which you are

seeking improvement. Alternately, you may choose to have the class name handicapped children they know. What can the class do to invite and include these people?

7. Read Matthew 25:31-40 aloud together. Pass out the Bible worksheet for this lesson, and allow the students time to fill in the blanks. Close by discussing the passage together.

The Least Of These

Matthew 25:31-40 — *The Good News Bible (Today's English Version)*

[31] "When the _____ of Man comes as _____ and all the angels with him, he will sit on his royal _____, [32] and the people of all the _____ will be gathered before him. Then he will _____ them into _____ groups, just as a _____ separates the _____ from the _____. [33] He will put the _____ people at his right and the others at his left. [34] Then the King will say to the people on his _____, 'Come, you that are _____ by my Father! Come, and possess the _____ which has been prepared for you ever since the _____ of the _____. [35] I was _____ and you _____ me, _____ and you gave me a _____; I was a _____ and you received me in your homes, [36] naked and you _____ me; I was _____ and you took care of me, in _____ and you visited me.' [37] The righteous will then answer him, 'When, Lord, did we ever see you hungry and _____ you, or thirsty and give you a _____? [38] When did we ever see you a _____ and welcome you in our homes, or _____ and clothe you? [39] When did we ever see you _____ or in _____, and visit you?' [40] The King will reply, 'I tell you, _____ you did this for one of the _____ important of these _____ of mine, you did it for _____!' "

Key

The Least Of These

Matthew 25:31-40 — *The Good News Bible (Today's English Version)*

³¹ *"When the* __Son__ *of Man comes as* __King__ *and all the angels with him, he will sit on his royal* __throne__ *,* ³² *and the people of all the* __nations__ *will be gathered before him. Then he will* __divide__ *them into* __two__ *groups, just as a* __shepherd__ *separates the* __sheep__ *from the* __goats__ *.* ³³ *He will put the* __righteous__ *people at his right and the others at his left.* ³⁴ *Then the King will say to the people on his* __right__ *, 'Come, you that are* __blessed__ *by my Father! Come, and possess the* __kingdom__ *which has been prepared for you ever since the* __creation__ *of the* __world__ *.* ³⁵ *I was* __hungry__ *and you* __fed__ *me,* __thirsty__ *and you gave me a* __drink__ *; I was a* __stranger__ *and you received me in your homes,* ³⁶ *naked and you* __clothed__ *me; I was* __sick__ *and you took care of me, in* __prison__ *and you visited me.'* ³⁷ *The righteous will then answer him, 'When, Lord, did we ever see you hungry and* __feed__ *you, or thirsty and give you a* __drink__ *?* ³⁸ *When did we ever see you a* __stranger__ *and welcome you in our homes, or* __naked__ *and clothe you?* ³⁹ *When did we ever see you* __sick__ *or in* __prison__ *, and visit you?'* ⁴⁰ *The King will reply, 'I tell you,* __whenever__ *you did this for one of the* __least__ *important of these* __brothers__ *of mine, you did it for* __me__ *!' "*

Session 11
Let's Look At Us
by Ralph Karstedt

PURPOSE:
To help students understand their own limitations (handicaps) as well as their abilities.

MATERIALS:
>   Paper
>   Crayons, markers, colored pencils
>   Chalkboard or newsprint chart

PROCEDURE:
1. Give each student paper and drawing materials. Invite them to draw a picture of something they would like to do if only they could.

2. Have each student show and explain his or her picture to the class. Look for the self-limitation revealed in each drawing. (For example: A person wishing he could jump tall buildings like Superman is suggesting he isn't as powerful or mobile as he would like to be.) The teacher should take time in this activity. Use a chalkboard or newsprint chart to list the limitations (handicaps) suggested.

3. Explain to the class that we all have things we cannot do or be. These are our own "handicaps."

4. Read Matthew 9:27-31, Mark 7:32-35, and Luke 13:10-13. In these Jesus causes blind people to see, the deaf to hear, and the lame to walk. Discuss the question *"How does God help handicapped people today?"* You may want to talk about eyeglasses, Braille, sign language, wheelchairs, canes, hearing aids, and so on.

5. Tell the class this story:
A certain man had a wonderful dog who could walk on water. When a new minister came to town, the man took the pastor hunting with him and the dog. When he shot a bird, the man said, "Fetch," and the dog walked out and picked it up. This happened three times.

Each time the minister said nothing. Finally the man looked at the minister and said, "Don't you notice something unusual about my dog?"

"Yes," the minister replied, "he can't swim, can he?"

Ask the class why we always think of the things a person *can't* do. Show the class the following figure, or draw it on the board:

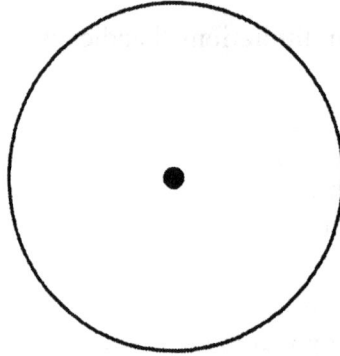

Ask the class what they see. Most persons respond by saying ONLY there is a black dot in the middle of the circle. Why? The dot is so much smaller than the large portion of the circle which is white.

Now invite each student to draw a picture and tell of something he or she can do very well. You may wish to display these next to the first drawings on a wall or bulletin board in your room.

6. Close with a prayer circle. As the teacher you may wish to take a moment to go around the circle and comment on a special ability or gift you have noticed in each of the students. Finish by allowing those in the circle to thank God for a unique ability they have been given.

Session 12
What Does It Mean To Be "Healed"?
by David and Carol Black

PURPOSE:

1. To allow students to explore biblical stories through the use of role-play.

2. To begin to make connections between Jesus' compassion in scripture and our own attitudes toward others.

3. To teach students that the power of God in Jesus as demonstrated by biblical stories of healing is not limited to individual acts of "healing." Rather, it is displayed through the lives of those who see and are changed by the miracle of love and the power of Christ.

MATERIALS NEEDED:

      Cot or board to be used as a litter

      Soft cloth bands, belts, or ropes for binding

PROCEDURE:

Bible Role-Play #1

Read Mark 2:2-12. Have students role-play the story, binding one of the students to the cot or litter, so he or she cannot move. Carefully carry the cot up stairs, and have students lower the cot from a table to demonstrate how it must be done. Afterwards have the "paralyzed man" tell how it felt not to be able to move as these events took place. Ask the students who carried the cot and lowered it what it was like to have to perform tasks like these.

DISCUSSION:

Discuss the fact that, while Jesus did heal this particular man from his infirmity, he healed the man's spirit first. Some students may have heard of the old biblical concept that disease or infirmity was caused by sin, and these afflictions were punishments from God. Remind them that Jesus first forgave the sins of the paralyzed man, demonstrating that he had the authority to do this. It was only when the Pharisees demanded that he prove his authority that Jesus told the man to get up and walk.

Also allow the students to explore the possible feelings of the gathered crowd or the helping friends at the moment that Jesus stopped his teaching, interrupted what he was doing, and focused on the paralyzed man. Jesus changed his own "agenda" to accommodate this need.

Bible Role-Play #2

Read Acts 3:1-10. Let volunteers role-play the story, or act it out as a narrator reads. If your class is large, divide the group into smaller groups and let each group bring its own interpretation of the story to the class. After several children have had an opportunity to be the main characters, have the students discuss how they felt if they were the lame person, or if they were one of the apostles.

DISCUSSION:

Please emphasize to the students that Jesus did not heal people because he only liked to be with them if they were "whole" persons. Jesus met with and fellowshiped with people of all varieties, regardless of pressure from the society of his time. Matthew, one of his disciples, was a tax collector; Zacchaeus was a tax collector, a thief, and small enough in stature to have that be an identifying characteristic; the woman at the well was a Samaritan. Jesus continually met people "where they were," and worked to touch spirit, mind, and body with new life. This power attracted others to him.

The result of the activity of healing is that people are filled with wonder and amazement (v. 10). The very name of Jesus has the power to make people see their world and others in a brand-new way.

CLOSING:

Ask the class to form a circle and offer a prayer of thanksgiving to God for caring enough to want to make us whole in all ways. Also pray for the ability to encounter and accept each other just the way we are — full of God's potential and grace.

Session 13
Receive This Gift ...
by Sherrie and Bill Drake

PURPOSE:

1. To demonstrate to children that all persons have gifts of value that need to be offered and need to be accepted.

2. To demonstrate that it is easy for people to discriminate for very silly reasons.

MATERIALS:

>Blank index cards
>Colored "garage sale" pricing dots (red, blue, and yellow)

ACTIVITY:

"Let's Make A Deal" Game

Construct enough cards that you have one for each student, and equal numbers of red, blue, and yellow dotted cards. Shuffle cards and then fold the dots inside the card so they cannot be readily seen.

As students arrive in the classroom, hand each an index card. When all students have arrived, tell students they are to exchange cards with each other, but no one is to have his or her original card when trading is finished. Then explain that the object of the trading is to try to get a card with a red dot. If they cannot negotiate that, a blue dot will be acceptable. Don't even acknowledge that there are yellow dots available. Emphasize only the two "desirable" cards to have.

Allow enough time for trading. Gather for discussion.

DISCUSSION:

At the beginning of the activity, students with yellow dots wished to trade for blue or red. Those with blue or red should have refused to trade with students with yellow dots. As you begin the discussion, ask those with yellow dots how they felt when they had something that no one would accept. Ask those with blue and red if they got annoyed with the insistence of the yellow in their attempts to trade something not acceptable as "trade-worthy." It is often very difficult for persons with disabilities to find opportunities to share their gifts in the church. Even though they have gifts of music, drama, speaking, teaching, ushering, serving, and so forth, they are frequently dismissed thoughtlessly because of their disability.

Discuss the basic social needs of "belonging to the group," "being cared for," and "being needed." Everyone needs to feel a sense of belonging, being needed, and feeling they are cared for by those around them. Students might draw invitations to Sunday school for the next week for someone they would like to see included who might be ignored for some reason the class has discussed.

59

BIBLE STUDY:

1 Corinthians 12:12-18. Have a volunteer read this passage. Discuss with the children how it might feel to be "just a nostril" or "just an eyelid" or another body part. Let that lead into a discussion of the necessity for all parts of the body, and the subsequent loss to the body of that part and what adjustments would be needed to get along without it. Help the children to a realization that every part of the body is needed, and that when parts cannot function optimally, they may atrophy and the body may lose that portion. Help the children realize that the church is like a body that needs all of its parts. When persons with disabilities are not allowed to contribute, the whole suffers.

OPTIONAL ACTIVITY:

If there is time during the Bible study, have a volunteer lie on his or her back on the floor on top of a large sheet of butcher paper (or some other large, single sheet). Use a crayon or marker to outline the body onto the paper.

While looking at the outline, guide the class through thinking what the different parts of the body might contribute to the whole. For example, the head might contribute ideas. The heart might be where feelings of kindness and thoughtfulness could be located. Hands might be creative. Feet might be strong, and so on.

After your class has generated ideas, use one or more of the following discussion questions. *(Please note that the apostle Paul gives you a ready answer for any child who might think it's funny to nominate himself/herself or another child as a body part that's not readily mentioned in polite society. Paul indicates that those parts should be treated with the most honor!)*

    1. If you could choose, which part of the body would you like to be?

    2. In our class, who do you think acts for us like a head, hand, foot, and so forth?

    3. Do you know people in our church who fill these different roles for the church?

CLOSING:

Close with prayer for the strength we get being part of a "body" whose "whole is greater than the sum of its parts."

Extra Activity
Accessibility Scavenger Hunt
by Suzanne Mades

PHYSICAL DISABILITY

1. Is there an accessible entrance where there are no stairs?
2. If the building has more than one floor, is there an elevator? Are there stops at every level of the building?
3. Does the bathroom have enough room for a wheelchair to turn? Is there at least 42 inches between the stool and the wall? Is the stall at least 42 inches wide?
4. Can wheelchair users reach the fire alarm and telephone?
5. Are there spaces in the sanctuary where wheelchair users can sit without sticking out into an aisle?
6. Is the chancel area (where the altar is) accessible to wheelchair users?
7. Are all exterior doors a minimum of 36 inches wide and interior doors a minimum of 32 inches wide?
8. Do doors have levers rather than round knobs?

VISUAL IMPAIRMENTS

1. Are there large print bulletins?
2. Are there large print hymnals?
3. Are there Braille signs for rooms?
4. Does the elevator have Braille buttons or tactile symbols to indicate floors?

DEAFNESS

1. Is the worship service interpreted in sign language?
2. Do any congregation members know enough sign language to greet and welcome a deaf person to the congregation?
3. Are there flashing lights for alarms so deaf people will know there is a fire?
4. Is there a telecommunication device for the deaf (TDD) available for deaf people to make telephone calls?

HARD OF HEARING

1. Are there Assistive Listening Devices available during worship?
2. Do phones have a button to push to increase the volume?

GENERAL

1. Are at least two of every fifty parking spaces reserved with a sign for persons with disabilities?
2. Are the parking spaces at least 96 inches wide and an adjacent aisle of 60 inches wide?

Additional Resources

Video Resources

Animals Need Good Feelings, Too (Program 1) 1990
> Approximately fifteen minutes: Handicapped birds and animals provide lessons in both science and self-esteem building, with topics for discussion, including dares, teasing, showing off, jealousy.
> *Available from North Indiana Conference Media Resource Center.*

Kathy: On My Own 1996
> 23 minutes: Kathy is handicapped, but like all teenagers she dreams of the day she would be on her own. She wants a chance for true independence and total self-reliance. To Kathy, taking that step would be one of life's biggest triumphs.
> *Available from North Indiana Conference Media Resource Center.*

Good Friends
Let's Be Friends — Joni Erickson Tada
Meet My Friends — Joni Erickson Tada
There's No One Exactly Like Me
> Copies of these videos are available at the North Indiana Conference Office for use by those churches utilizing this curriculum.

Stories To Read

Bein' With You This Way — Lisa W. Nikola
Charlsie's Chuckle — Clara Berkus
Hope For The Flowers — Triva Paulus
My Brother, Matthew — Mary Thompson
The Tree That Survived The Winter — Mary Fahy

Further Resources For Adults

Circles Of Friends Series — Robert Perske
> *Don't Stop The Music*
> *Hope For The Families*
> *New Life In The Neighborhood*
> *Show Me No Mercy*
> *Earn Equal Justice*

Honor Thy Son — Lou Shaw
The Disabled God: Toward A Liberatory Theology Of Disability — Nancy Risland

Sunday School Curriculum

Bridges — a resource for the adaptation of United Methodist Sunday School curriculum for persons with disabilities. Free sample packet available.

All of the above available through Cokesbury (800) 672-1789

Resources For Worship
(Using disabilities as the theme)
by Robert S. Jarboe

About The Enclosed Song
("Holy God, Help Us Love Each Other")

This song (or hymn) was written for use with this curriculum and worship service. Enclosed you will find three copies:

    1. Chorus for use in the worship bulletin
    2. Soloist's copy
    3. Accompanist's copy

This song may be used in four ways:

    1. Performed as a solo
    2. Performed as a choral anthem
    3. Children learn the chorus and
        a. Choir sings the verses or
        b. Soloist sings the verses or
        c. Each Sunday School class sings a verse
    4. Congregation sings the chorus and
        a. Choir sings the verses or
        b. Soloist sings the verses or
        c. Each Sunday School class sings a verse

Copyright permission: Permission is granted to make copies for the sole use of the Sunday School curriculum or the worship service. The title and name of the composer must be included in each copy.

Suggested Hymns from the United Methodist Hymnal

#182 — "Word of God, Come Down to Earth"
#191 — "Jesus Loves Me! This I Know"
#256 — "We Would See Jesus"
       (Alternate tune: "O Perfect Love")
#262 — "Heal Me, Hands of Jesus"
#263 — "When Jesus the Healer Passed Through Galilee"
#265 — "O Christ, the Healer"
       (Alternate tunes: "Lord, Speak to Me"
                 "Come Sinners, to the Gospel Feast")
#266 — "Heal Us, Emmanuel, Hear Our Prayer"
       (Alternate tunes: "Must Jesus Bear the Cross Alone?"
                 "Jesus, the Very Thought of Thee")
#375 — "There is a Balm in Gilead"
#382 — "Have Thine Own Way, Lord"
#458 — "Dear Lord, for All in Pain"

Call To Worship

Leader: We come as we are,
      from different walks of life
      and ways of life.
People: We come to worship our glorious God
      who loves us with our abilities
      and disabilities.
Leader: Worship, then, God who is gracious to us.

Prayer Of Confession

We confess to you, O God, our vanity and pride
      when we use our abilities for our own gain,
      for they become disabilities for your Kingdom.
When we realize our disabilities
      and yet still strive to serve you,
      they become abilities.
Forgive us when we fail to realize your Will
      for our lives.
Send your Spirit
      that we may be humble with our abilities
      and strengthened with our disabilities
      to your glory and honor. Amen.

Benediction

Go forth as healed people,
      knowing that the Trinity God
      has brought you healing wholeness.
      Go forth in praise. Amen.

Eucharist Service

The Lord be with you.
      And also with you.
Lift up your hearts.
      We lift them up to the Lord.
Let us give thanks to the Lord our God.
      It is right to give our thanks and praise.
It is right, and a good and joyful thing
      always and everywhere to give thanks
      to you, Almighty God,
      Creator of heaven and earth.

You worked your Will through your people
   despite their disabilities,
   such as Moses with his stammering and
   Jacob with his limping,
   as well as Paul with his "thorn in the flesh."

And so, with your people on earth
   and all the company of heaven,
   we praise your name and join
   their unending hymn:

Holy, holy, holy Lord,
   God of power and might,
   heaven and earth are full of your glory.
Hosanna in the highest.
Blessed is he who comes
   in the name of the Lord.
Hosanna in the highest.

Holy are you,
   and blessed is your Son Jesus Christ.
He healed those who came to him with their
   disabilities and showed to all a
   Kingdom where all would ultimately
   be healed as well.

By the baptism of his suffering, death,
   and resurrection,
   you gave birth to your church,
   delivered us from slavery to sin and death,
   and made with us a new covenant
   by water and the Spirit.

On the night in which he gave himself up for us
   he took bread, gave thanks to you,
   broke the bread,
   gave it to his disciples, and said,
   "Take, eat; this is my body which is given for you.
   Do this in remembrance of me."

When the supper was over
   he took the cup,
   gave thanks to you,
   gave it to his disciples, and said,

"Drink from this, all of you,
this is my blood of the new covenant
poured out for you and for many
for the forgiveness of sins.
Do this, as often as you drink it,
in remembrance of me."

And so,
in remembrance of these your mighty acts
in Jesus Christ,
we offer ourselves in praise and thanksgiving
as a holy and living sacrifice,
in union with Christ's offering for us,
as we proclaim the mystery of faith.

Christ has died; Christ is risen; Christ will come again.

Pour our your Holy Spirit on us,
gathered here,
and on these gifts of bread and wine.
Make them be for us
the body and blood of Christ,
that we may be for the world
the body of Christ, redeemed by his blood
that all will be perfect in all ways when we come
together in your Kingdom.

(Intercession may be added)

By your spirit make us one with Christ,
one with each other,
and one in ministry to all the world,
until Christ comes in final victory
and we feast at the heavenly banquet.

Through your Son, Jesus Christ,
with the Holy Spirit in your holy church,
all honor and glory is yours,
almighty God, now and forever. **Amen.**

And now with the confidence of children
of God, we are bold to pray:

Our Father, who art in heaven,
   hallowed by thy name.
   Thy kingdom come,
   thy Will be done on earth as it is in heaven.
   Give us this day our daily bread.
   And forgive us our trespasses
   as we forgive those who trespass against us.
   And lead us not into temptation,
   but deliver us from evil.
   For thine is the kingdom, and the power,
   and the glory, forever. Amen.

(The pastor breaks the bread while saying)
Because there is one loaf,
   we, who are many, are one body,
   for we all partake of the one loaf.
The bread which we break
   is a sharing in the body of Christ.

(The pastor lifts the cup while saying)
The cup over which we give thanks
   is a sharing in the blood of Christ.

(The bread and cup are given to the people with these words)
The body of Christ given for you. **Amen.**
The blood of Christ given for you. **Amen.**

Eternal God,
   we give thanks for this holy mystery
   in which you have given yourself to us.
We pray that you instill within us your
   Holy Spirit, that we may respond to your
   call with no regard to our
   abilities or disabilities.
Grant that we may go into the world
   in the strength of your Spirit,
   to give ourselves for others,
   in the name of Jesus Christ our Lord. **Amen.**

Holy God, Help Us Love Each Other

R.S.J.

Robert S. Jarboe

Lyrics under staves:

chorus: Ho - ly God, help us love each o - ther;

those we know and those from a - far.

All that we do or can't for You, we

know You love us just as we are.

F   C   F   F(add2)   F   C   G7

1. May we ne - ver hin - der each o - ther
2. See - ing, hear - ing, your great cre - a - tion
3. Walk - ing, run - ning, glid - ing in wheel - chair,
4. You have called us to be your chil - dren

F   Em   Am   Dm7   G7

sing - ing dif' - rent ways.
ways that we ob - serve.
crutch - es, walk - ers too;
serv - ing dif' - rent ways.

F   G7   C   C   F   C

With our mouths and hands we give to you
Know - ing that You love we each one of us,
tho we're dif - rent, we each have u - ni - ty
How we do it, it's our best for You

F   C   F   Em   Dm7   C7/G

ho - nor, glo - ry and praise.
we are all called to serve.
mov - ing for - ward for You.
Bless us now with your grace.   *to chorus*

71

Holy God, Help Us Love Each Other

R.S.J.   Robert S. Jarboe

chorus

Ho - ly God, help us love each o - ther;

Those we know and those from a - far.

All that we do or can't for You, we

know You love us just as we are.

1. May we ne - ver hin - der each o - ther
2. See - ing, hear - ing, your great cre - a - tion
3. Walk - ing, run - ning, glid - ing in wheel - chair,
4. You have called us to be your chil - dren

sing - ing dif - rent ways;
ways that we ob - serve.
crutch - es, walk - ers too;
serv - ing dif - rent ways.

With our mouths and hands we give to You
Know - ing that You love each one of us,
Tho we're dif - rent, we have u - ni - ty
How we do it, it's our best for You.

Ho - nor, glo - ry and praise.
we are all called to serve.
mov - ing for - ward for You.
Bless us now with your grace.

(c)1996 R.S.Jarboe

Holy God, Help Us Love Each Other

R.S.J.   Robert S. Jarboe

Ho - ly God, help us love each o - ther;
those we know and those from a - far.
All that we do or can't for You, we
know You love us just as we are.

(c)1996 R.S.Jarboe

NOTE: The above chorus may be copied and inserted into the
worship service of a legal or letter size bulletin should you
desire the congregation to sing the chorus. The title may be
omitted, but the composer name and copyright should still be
included. Remember, you have permission to copy any of
this music for your worship purposes.

www.ingramcontent.com/pod-product-compliance
Lightning Source LLC
Chambersburg PA
CBHW050356100426
42739CB00015BB/3419